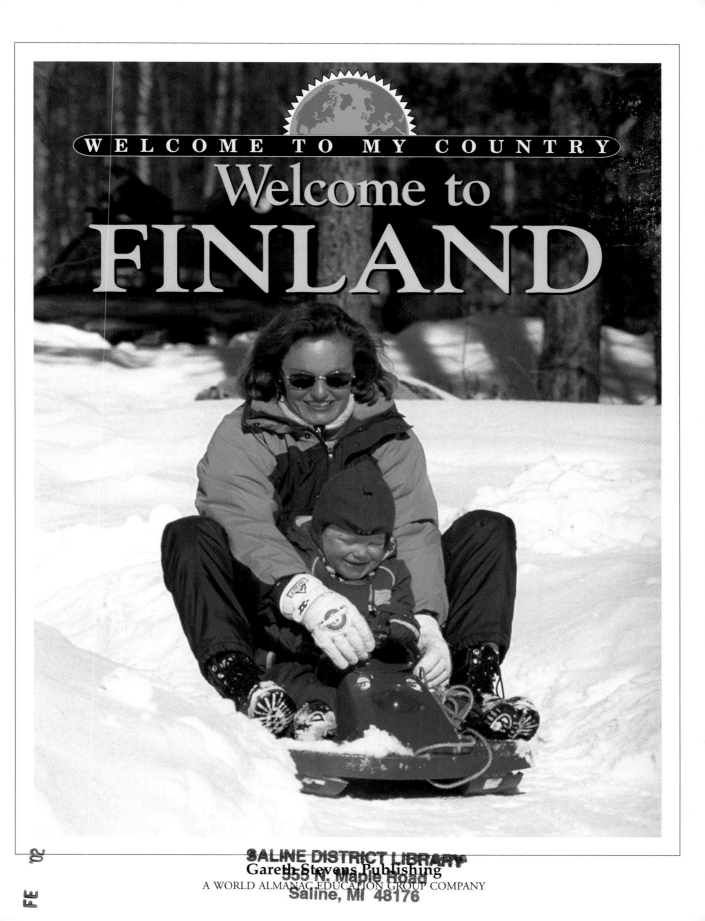

WELCOME TO MY COUNTRY

Welcome to
FINLAND

Gareth Stevens Publishing
A WORLD ALMANAC EDUCATION GROUP COMPANY

Written by
DORA YIP/ZHONG MEICHUN

Edited in USA by
ALAN WACHTEL

Designed by
JAILANI BASARI

Picture research by
SUSAN JANE MANUEL

First published in North America in 2002 by
Gareth Stevens Publishing
A World Almanac Education Group Company
330 West Olive Street, Suite 100
Milwaukee, Wisconsin 53212 USA

Please visit our web site at:
www.garethstevens.com
For a free color catalog describing
Gareth Stevens' list of high-quality books
and multimedia programs, call
1-800-542-2595 (USA) or
1-800-461-9120 (CANADA).
Gareth Stevens Publishing's
Fax: (414) 332-3567.

© **TIMES MEDIA PRIVATE LIMITED 2002**
Originated and designed by
Times Editions
An imprint of Times Media Private Limited
A member of the Times Publishing Group
Times Centre, 1 New Industrial Road
Singapore 536196
http://www.timesone.com.sg/te

Library of Congress Cataloging-in-Publication Data
Yip, Dora.
Welcome to Finland / Dora Yip and Zhong Meichun.
p. cm.— (Welcome to my country)
Includes bibliographical references and index.
Summary: An overview of the geography, history, government,
economy, people, and culture of Finland.
ISBN 0-8368-2531-4 (lib. bdg.)
1. Finland—Juvenile literature. [1. Finland.] I. Zhong, Meichun.
II. Title. III. Series.
DL1012.Y56   2002
948.97—dc21   2001042014

Printed in Malaysia

1 2 3 4 5 6 7 8 9 06 05 04 03 02

PICTURE CREDITS
A.N.A. Press Agency: 36, 41 (bottom)
Bes Stock: 18
Stefano Cellai: 45
Comma Finland: Cover, 1, 3 (top), 3
  (center), 5, 8, 20, 21, 22, 23, 34, 38, 43
Robert Fried: 2, 6, 10, 26, 29 (bottom), 30,
  33, 35 (top)
HBL Network: 4, 16, 39 (bottom), 40
Dave G. Houser: 28, 41 (top)
Jason Lauré: 19
Lehtikuva Oy: 7, 9 (both), 12, 13 (both), 14,
  15 (all), 24, 25, 29 (top), 31 (both), 32,
  35 (bottom), 39 (top)
Nik Wheeler: 3 (bottom), 11 (both), 17,
  27 (both), 37

Digital Scanning by Superskill Graphics Pte Ltd

Contents

Words that appear in the glossary are printed in **boldface** type the first time they occur in the text.

Welcome to Finland!

Finland is often called "the country of thousands of lakes." It is a land of great beauty and a paradise for nature lovers. Finland is also very advanced in **telecommunications** and other kinds of electronic **technology**. Let's explore Finland and learn about its people, history, and culture.

Opposite: Finns love to fish, both in summer and winter.

Below: These Finnish girls are ready for a hike on a nature trail.

The Flag of Finland

The Finnish national flag has a blue cross on a white background. A poet once suggested that the colors of the flag stand for the blue of Finland's lakes and the white snow of its winters. Finland adopted this flag in 1919.

The Land

With an area of 130,128 square miles (337,032 square kilometers), Finland is the fifth largest country in Europe. Almost one-third of its land lies north of the Arctic Circle.

The Russian Federation is east of Finland, Sweden is to the west, and Norway is to the north. More than 30,000 small islands are found off the southern and western coastlines.

Below: The Åland **archipelago** lies between Finland and Sweden. With 6,500 islands, it is the biggest island chain in the country. Some of the islands are very popular with tourists.

Forests cover more than three-quarters of Finland, and the country has more than 187,000 lakes. The low, flat land on the southern and western coasts has fertile soil, which makes it excellent for farming.

The area furthest north is called Lapland. All of Finland's mountains are in northwestern Lapland. The highest mountain is Haltiatunturi, at 4,344 feet (1,324 meters).

Above: Many of Finland's lakes are surrounded by pine, spruce, and birch trees.

Climate

Finland has a cold climate. Winters are long, with temperatures as low as −22° Fahrenheit (−3° Celsius) in the north and −4° F (−20° C) in the south. High temperatures reach 80° F (27° C) in the north, 72° F (22° C) in the south.

Far above the Arctic Circle, parts of Finland have two straight months of darkness in winter and two straight months of daylight in summer.

Above: In Finland, snow starts to fall in October and does not begin to melt until April.

Plants and Animals

Pine and spruce are the two main types of trees in Finland's forests. Forest wildlife includes lynxes, wolves, and foxes. Finland's largest animal, the brown bear, is an **endangered** species.

At least three hundred bird species live in Finland, and more than seventy kinds of fish, including salmon and herring, are found in Finland's lakes.

Above: Prickly thistle plants grow wild all over Finland. Their silky flowers are usually pink.

Left: Wolverines live in the cold northern areas of Finland. They are part of the weasel family, but they look like small bears, and they smell like skunks.

History

The Finno-Ugric peoples, who came from what is now central Russia, were among the earliest settlers in Finland. Other Europeans also came to live in Finland. Because the many different groups of settlers did not form a single nation, the neighboring countries of Sweden and Russia fought for control of Finland. Sweden gradually won.

Below: In 1280, the Finns built Turku Castle to protect them from their enemies. Turku was the capital of Finland until 1808.

Left:
These eighteenth-century cannons are in Suomenlinna Fortress. The Finns built this fortress to guard the sea around Helsinki, Finland's capital city.

Swedish Rule

Christian **missionaries** from Sweden arrived in Finland in 1155, and many other Swedes followed. Then, in 1323, Sweden and Russia signed the **Treaty** of Nöteborg, making most of Finland part of Sweden. The Swedes gave the Finns equal rights and self-rule, and they helped develop the country's economy. Between 1500 and 1790, however, Sweden and Russia fought more wars for control of Finland.

Below:
This monument **commemorates** Gustave III (1746–1792), a Swedish king who also ruled Finland. He encouraged Finland to trade with other nations.

11

Russian Rule

In 1809, Russia took control of Finland. At first, the Finns were allowed to speak their own language and make their own laws. Then, in the 1890s, Russia took away those freedoms. The Finns were ready to go to war against Russia, but the Russian Revolution of 1917 gave Finland the opportunity to declare its independence without a fight.

Above: Finland's independence from Russia, declared on December 6, 1917, is remembered in the city of Helsinki by burning torches. The statue in the background is Carl Gustaf Emil Mannerheim, a hero of the Winter War of 1939.

Soviet Rule

The **Soviet Union** took over Finland in the Winter War of 1939. The Finns did not accept Soviet rule, so Finland let the Germans cross their land to attack the Soviets during World War II. The Soviet Union **retaliated** by attacking Finland.

When Finland and the Soviet Union finally made peace in 1944, Finland had to give part of its land to the Soviet Union and pay war **reparations** to the Soviets. Finland was badly damaged and in debt but was finally independent.

Left:
Some Finnish soldiers fought on skis against the Soviet Union during the Winter War of 1939.

Modern Finland

Today, Finland is a **neutral** country. It has been a member of the United Nations since 1955 and has friendly relations and trade agreements with all nations, especially Scandinavian countries and Russia (part of the former Soviet Union). Although the breakup of the Soviet Union in the late 1980s hurt Finland's economy, it was strong again by 1995.

Below:
Urho Kekkonen (1900 –1986) was Finland's president from 1956 to 1974. A skillful **diplomat**, Kekkonen helped keep Finland out of conflicts with other nations.

Elias Lönnrot (1802–1884)

Elias Lönnrot **compiled** Finnish folk songs and poems into a book called the *Kalevala*, or *Land of Heroes*. It is Finland's national folk **epic**.

Elias Lönnrot

Minna Canth (1844–1897)

Minna Canth was a well-known feminist playwright. Her plays describe the roles of women and workers in Finnish society.

Carl Gustaf Emil Mannerheim (1867–1951)

Mannerheim is considered the greatest general in Finnish history. He was also Finland's president from 1944 to 1946.

Carl Mannerheim

Paavo Nurmi (1897–1973)

Long-distance runner Paavo Nurmi, known as the Flying Finn, won nine Olympic gold medals in the 1920s.

Paavo Nurmi

Government and the Economy

Finland is a democratic **republic** with a president and a parliament. The president, who is elected to a six-year term, is the head of state and has broad **executive** power. The Parliament is led by a prime minister who is appointed by the president. The Parliament has 200 elected members. Each member serves a four-year term.

Below: The Finnish Parliament building is in Helsinki.

The justice system in Finland includes both independent courts and an officer called an ombudsman, who reviews citizens' complaints against the government.

Finland's six provinces and more than 450 **municipalities** have local governments. Each province has a governor chosen by the president, and each municipality elects a council that manages services such as electricity.

Above: The Town Hall in Porvoo, a town northeast of Helsinki, was the meeting place of Finland's first government.

Economy

In the past, Finland's economy was based on agriculture. Today, less than one-tenth of the land is used for farming. Since World War II, Finland has been an industrial nation.

Forests are the country's most valuable natural resource. Mineral deposits, such as zinc, iron ore, and copper are also important resources.

Above: Factories line the waterfront in Tampere, a major industrial city in Western Finland.

Although its main industries are forest products, engineering, and electronics, Finland is also a world leader in mining technology and **metallurgy**. Other important industries are chemicals, textiles, and food.

Major exports include electrical and telecommunications equipment and pulp and paper. Main trading partners are Germany, Sweden, the United Kingdom, the United States, and the Russian Federation.

Below: Finnish factories produce many household goods, such as enamel cookware.

People and Lifestyle

With just over five million people, Finland's population is one of the smallest in Europe. Almost everyone who lives in Finland was born there.

Finland's main **ethnic** minority groups are the Sami and the Romany. The Sami were the first people to live there. Today, about 5,700 Sami live in

Below: Many Finns have blonde hair, blue eyes, and fair skin. They inherit these features from their Scandinavian ancestors.

the province of Lapland. About 6,500 Romany people, or Gypsies, live throughout the country.

Finns are known for their honesty and strong character. They take pride in being able to survive through times of trouble. *Sisu* (SEE-soo), a Finnish word that means independent, courageous, and strong, defines the ideal Finn. Finns speak quietly, value their privacy, and rarely show affection in public.

Above: Because Finns value privacy, many of them have second homes or summer cottages in areas away from the cities or near one of the country's many lakes.

Family Life

Finnish families are small, usually with only one or two children. Often, both parents have jobs, and they make most family decisions together. Wives usually do the housework, but with some help from their husbands.

A newborn baby gets a lot of attention. Family and friends come to visit the baby and bring food, clothes, and other gifts to celebrate the birth.

Above: Finnish families like to spend weekends together. Weekends in Finland usually include a lot of time outdoors.

The Roles of Men and Women

For the most part, Finnish men and women have equal status and are equally well-educated. They each make up half the workforce. About 70 percent of the female population works outside the home.

In farming areas, however, most men and women still have traditional roles. Men work in the fields. Women cook and clean and raise the children.

Below: Many Finnish women work outside the home. They value their independence and careers.

Education

Education in Finland is free, and all children between the ages of seven and sixteen attend **comprehensive school**. Parents may enroll their children in either a Finnish-language or a Swedish-language school.

Languages, especially English, Russian, French, and German are important in the country's educational system. Children study three foreign languages in comprehensive school.

Below: Schools run from 8:00 a.m. to 2:00 p.m. in Finland. Lunch is free, and some schools serve breakfast, too. In this picture, the teacher sits among his students.

After nine years of comprehensive school, students attend high school for three years or **vocational school** for two or three years. Students in vocational schools learn trade skills, such as hairdressing or auto mechanics.

High school graduates who pass an entrance examination may continue their education by studying at one of Finland's more than twenty universities or many **polytechnic** institutes.

Above: Every year, on the last Saturday in May, Finnish high school graduates receive certificates. All graduates wear white caps, and the young women also carry red roses.

Religion

Although many Finns do not go to church regularly, they celebrate special events in church, including baptisms, weddings, and funerals. Lutheran is Finland's official religion, but Finns are free to choose their religion.

The Evangelical Lutheran Church of Finland is the country's largest church, with more than four million members.

Above: Tampere Cathedral was designed by architect Lars Sonck in 1907.

The Eastern Orthodox Church, Finland's second-largest church, has only about fifty thousand members.

The state gives financial assistance to the Lutheran and Eastern Orthodox churches. State money pays for social service and educational programs. These church programs help the poor, the old, and the disabled.

Finland also has small groups of Jehovah's Witnesses, Adventists, Catholics, and Jews. Many other Finns do not belong to any religious group.

Above: Lumi Lina Snow Castle is built in the city of Kemi every winter. This chapel is part of the Snow Castle.

Left: Uspenski Cathedral in Helsinki is the largest Eastern Orthodox Church in Europe. It was built in 1868.

Language

Finland's two official languages are Finnish and Swedish. About 94 percent of the population speak mainly Finnish, and the rest speak mainly Swedish.

Finnish is a hard language for foreigners to learn because the same word is used for "he" and "she," and the articles "the" and "a" are rarely used.

Below: Finns love to read. The stores in Finland sell books written in Finnish, Swedish, German, and English.

Literature

Mikael Agricola was Finland's first writer. He wrote about Finnish culture and religion. Finland's most famous book is the *Kalevala*, an epic of myths and poems compiled by Elias Lönnrot in the 1800s. Twentieth-century writer Frans Eemil Sillanpää won the Nobel Prize for Literature, in 1939, for his novels about ordinary Finnish people.

Arts

Finnish artists have been inspired by their country's beautiful scenery, courageous people, folk poetry, and the stories in the *Kalevala*. They also have been influenced by Finland's relationships with other nations. When Finland was under Russian rule, the work of Finnish artists expressed their pride in and love of their country.

Below: "The Three Smiths," a statue by Felix Nylund (1878–1940), stands in the center of this busy street in Helsinki.

Left: This painting by Akseli Gallen-Kallela illustrates "The Defense of Sampo," a story in the *Kalevala*.

Above: Many buildings in Finnish cities have modern, practical architecture.

The Golden Age of Art

The Russian period was the golden age of Finnish art. One famous painter of this **era** is Akseli Gallen-Kallela (1865–1931), who was inspired by the *Kalevala*. His student, Hugo Simberg (1873–1917), painted watercolors based on folktales. The paintings from this era can be found in Finnish museums.

Music

Finnish music began as church and folk music. Today, Finns listen to all kinds of music, from classical to rock.

Fredrik Pacius (1809–1891), who wrote the first Finnish opera as well as the country's national anthem, was Finland's first well-known composer. Jean Sibelius (1865–1957), however, is Finland's greatest composer.

Above: In Finland, even babies are encouraged to appreciate music.

Theater and Dance

The first known drama performance in Finland was in Turku in the 1650s. Since then, Finns have become big theater fans. The country has more than forty professional theater groups, and half of the plays performed are written by Finnish playwrights.

Finns are big dance fans, too. The styles they enjoy include ballet, tango, and rock 'n' roll, as well as traditional folk dance.

Below: Street musicians perform in Helsinki.

33

Leisure

All kinds of outdoor activities are popular in Finland. Finns walk, run, cycle, swim and golf, and families often go on weekend picnics together.

Finland has twenty-nine nature **reserves** covering nearly one-third of the country. With their marked trails and footpaths and special areas for tents, they are great places for hiking and camping out.

Below: Some hiking trails in Finland overlook beautiful lakes.

Summer Sports

Finland's national sport, *pesäpallo* (pay-SAH-PARL-loh), is a summer sport played in rural areas and small towns. It is played a lot like American baseball. Many Finns also play soccer.

In the summer Olympics, Finland has had its greatest success in long-distance running. Together, Finnish runners Paavo Nurmi and Ville Ritola have won fourteen gold medals.

Above: Finns enjoy fresh barbecued fish after ice fishing, or fishing through holes cut in the ice over frozen lakes.

Winter Sports

During the long winters, many Finns enjoy sports such as snowboarding, skiing, and ski jumping. Ice skating, ice fishing, iceboating, and driving snowmobiles are also popular. Large groups of Finns ski together every

weekend in winter, and thousands take part in the 47-mile (75-kilometer) Finlandia cross-country skiing race.

Above: Finns are expert cross-country skiers.

Ice hockey is a favorite winter team sport. Finland has junior leagues for young players, and Finns play in the

European league. Finland's hockey team won the bronze medal in the 1998 Winter Olympics. Outstanding hockey players from Finland have joined professional teams in the European Hockey League and the National Hockey League of North America.

Above: Reindeer races are popular in Lapland, where reindeer are raised as livestock.

Staying Indoors

Finns enjoy many indoor activities during winter, too. Playing video games, watching television, and surfing the Internet are especially popular with young Finns.

Left: At Eastertime, girls dress up as witches and visit their neighbors to wish them well, hoping to receive candy in return.

Festivals

Every year, Finland celebrates the coming of spring with two holidays, Easter and *Vappu* (VAH-poo). For Easter, Finns decorate their homes with pussy willow, straw dolls, and colored eggs. *Vappu*, on May 1, is also known as May Day. Labor Day

Opposite: Independence Day colors light up a park in Helsinki.

is on May 1, too. Finns celebrate this national holiday with carnivals, parades, and concerts.

Finland's Independence Day, on December 6, is usually celebrated at home, where Finns light candles to honor the heroes of independence.

Christmas Eve is a major Finnish festival. Early in the day, Finns bake cookies and decorate the Christmas tree. Christmas Eve dinner is a special meal. On Christmas morning, families open gifts and attend church services.

Above: Santa Claus is said to live near Rovaniemi, a village in Lapland. Visitors from all over the world visit Lapland to see him.

Food

Finns usually eat the simple, healthy foods that are in season. Summer is the time for berries and vegetables. In fall, Finns eat wild mushrooms and meat. Fish, especially salmon or rainbow trout, is eaten all year round.

Porridge with milk and butter is the traditional Finnish breakfast, but today, most Finns prefer cereal,

Below:
Finnish markets tempt shoppers with attractive displays of food.

yogurt, or rye bread with cheese and sausage. They also like *pulla* (POO-lah), a bread made with cardamom and raisins and sprinkled with sugar.

Lunch is the biggest meal of the day. It includes salad; bread; a main course of fish, chicken, or meat with sauce; and a side dish of boiled rice, potatoes, or pasta. Finnish dinners are small and easy to prepare. Favorite foods are pizzas, hamburgers, fish sticks, and casseroles.

Above: Fish is an important part of the Finnish diet.

FINLAND

Above: Boats of all sizes travel on Finland's many lakes and rivers.

Åland A5
Åland Islands A5
Arctic Circle A2–D2

Baltic Sea A5

Eastern Finland
    C3–C5
Estonia B5–C5

Gulf of Bothnia
    A5–B3
Gulf of Finland
    B5–C5

Haltiatunturi B1

Helsinki B5

Kemi B3
Kemijoki River B2

Lapland B1–C3

Norway A2–C1

Oulu B3–C3

Porvoo B5

Rovaniemi B2
Russian Federation
    C1–D5

Saimaa Lake C5
Southern Finland
    B5–C5
Sweden A4–B1

Tampere B4
Turku B5

Western Finland
    B3–B5

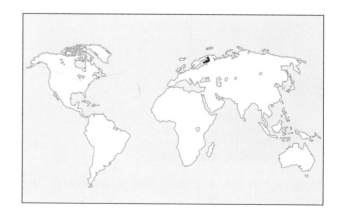

Quick Facts

Official Name	Republic of Finland
Capital	Helsinki
Official Languages	Finnish, Swedish
Population	5,167,486 (July 2000 estimate)
Land Area	130,128 square miles (337,032 square km)
Provinces	Åland, Eastern Finland, Lapland, Oulu, Southern Finland, Western Finland
Highest Point	Haltiatunturi (4,344 feet/1,324 m)
Ethnic Groups	Finnish, Swedish, Romany, Sami
Major Religions	Evangelical Lutheran, Eastern Orthodox
Important Festivals	Easter (March/April)
	Vappu (May Day)
	Midsummer (third weekend in June)
	Independence Day (December 6)
	Christmas (December 25)
Currency	markka (FIM 6.69 = U.S. $1 as of 2001)

Opposite: Since World War II, buildings in Helsinki have been designed to blend with their surroundings.

Glossary

archipelago: a group of many islands.

commemorates: remembers or calls to mind.

compiled: collected and organized.

comprehensive school: a school, such as an elementary school, that requires coursework in many subjects, or areas of knowledge.

diplomat: a government representative who deals with political problems in other countries.

endangered: in danger of dying out completely, or becoming extinct.

epic: a very long poem that describes extraordinary events or the deeds of a legendary or historical hero.

era: a period of time known for its distinctive characteristics or events.

ethnic: related to a certain race or culture of people.

executive: related to putting the laws of a state or a nation into effect and making sure they are carried out.

metallurgy: the process of separating metals from their ores.

missionaries: people who work to convert others to a particular religion.

municipalities: cities, towns, or villages with their own local governments.

neutral: not taking part in a dispute or a war between other countries.

polytechnic: related to education in technical subjects, such as industrial arts and applied sciences.

reparations: payment for damages.

republic: a country in which citizens elect their government representatives.

reserves: land set aside for special purposes, such as the preservation of nature or public use.

retaliated: returned an attack to get even for harm or injury.

Soviet Union: a communist nation, dissolved in 1991, that included Russia and fourteen other republics.

technology: science as it is used in everyday life.

telecommunications: technologies, such as telephone or the Internet, for communicating over a distance.

treaty: an agreement of peace and cooperation between two or more countries.

vocational school: a school that teaches the skills needed for particular jobs.

More Books to Read

Finland. Cultures of the World series.
    Tan Chung Lee
    (Benchmark Books)

Finland. Enchantment of the World
    series. Sylvia McNair
    (Children's Press)

Finland. Festivals of the World series.
    Tan Chung Lee (Gareth Stevens)

Finland. Major World Nations series.
    Alan James (Chelsea House)

Finland in Pictures. Mary M. Rodgers,
    editor (Lerner)

The Grandchildren of the Vikings. Reijo
    Harkonen and Matti A. Pitkanen
    (Carolrhoda Books)

*The Magic Storysinger: From the
    Finnish Epic Tale* Kalevala.
    M. E. A. McNeil (Stemmer House)

*The Maiden of Northland: A Hero
    Tale of Finland.* Aaron Shepard
    (Atheneum)

Scandinavia. Artisans Around the World
    series. Sharon Franklin et al
    (Raintree/Steck-Vaughn)

Videos

*Video Visits — Scandinavia: Land
    of the Midnight Sun.*
    (IVN Entertainment)

*Wild Europe — Tour the Natural
    Wonders of Wild Arctic.*
    (WGBH Boston)

Web Sites

www.gastrolab.net/c1gfinle.htm

www.publiscan.fi/

www.santaclausplaza.com/english/

www.scandinavica.com/sami.htm

www.tekdok.com/Finland/

Due to the dynamic nature of the Internet, some web sites stay current longer than
others. To find additional web sites, use a reliable search engine with one or more
of the following keywords to help you locate information about Finland. Keywords:
Åland, Haltiatunturi, Helsinki, Kalevala, Lapland, Sami, Santa Claus, Turku.

Index